[Page 4.]

"WELL, THEN, I SHALL HAVE TO TRUST YOU"

ILLUSTRATIONS

EVENING DRESS

Farce

BY

W. D. HOWELLS

ILLUSTRATED

NEW YORK

HARPER & BROTHERS PUBLISHERS

1893

Harper's "Black and White" Series.

Illustrated. 32mo, Cloth, 50 cents each.

EVENING DRESS. A Farce. By William Dean Howells.

THE WORK OF WASHINGTON IRVING. By Charles Dudley Warner.

EDWIN BOOTH. By Laurence Hutton.

THE DECISION OF THE COURT. A Comedy. By Brander Matthews.

PHILLIPS BROOKS. By Rev. Arthur Brooks, D.D.

GEORGE WILLIAM CURTIS. By John White Chadwick.

THE UNEXPECTED GUESTS. A Farce. By William Dean Howells.

SLAVERY AND THE SLAVE TRADE IN AFRICA. By Henry M. Stanley.

THE RIVALS. By François Coppée.

THE JAPANESE BRIDE. By Naomi Tamura.

WHITTIER: NOTES OF HIS LIFE AND OF HIS FRIENDSHIPS. By Annie Fields.

GILES COREY, YEOMAN. By Mary E. Wilkins.

COFFEE AND REPARTEE. By John Kendrick Bangs.

JAMES RUSSELL LOWELL. An Address. By George William Curtis.

SEEN FROM THE SADDLE. By Isa Carrington Cabell.

A FAMILY CANOE TRIP. By Florence Watters Snedeker.

A LITTLE SWISS SOJOURN. By William Dean Howells.

A LETTER OF INTRODUCTION. A Farce. By William Dean Howells.

IN THE VESTIBULE LIMITED. By Brander Matthews.

THE ALBANY DEPOT. A Farce. By William Dean Howells.

PUBLISHED BY HARPER & BROTHERS, NEW YORK.

For sale by all booksellers, or will be sent by the publishers, postage prepaid, on receipt of price.

EVENING DRESS

FARCE

I

*M*RS. EDWARD ROBERTS: "Now,
my dear, Amy and I will get there
early, so as to make up for your coming
a little late, but you *must* be there for
the last half, at least. I would excuse
you altogether if I could, for I know you
must be dead tired, up all night, that
way, on the train, but Mrs. Miller is one
of those people who never *can* listen to
reason, and she would take deadly offence if you missed her musicale, and
wouldn't forgive us the longest day she

lived. So you see?" Mrs. Roberts addresses herself to her husband in the library of their apartment in Hotel Bellingham, at Boston, as she stands before the fire pulling on a long glove and looking at him across his desk, where he has sunk into a weary heap in his swivel chair. "You *are* dreadfully used up, Edward, and I think it's cruel to make you go out; but what can I do? If it was anybody but Mrs. Miller I wouldn't *think* of having you go; I'm sure I never want to have her about, anyway. But that's just the kind of people that you're a perfect slave to! Now, dear, I've let the two girls go out, and you must remember that you're in the place alone with the children; but you needn't be troubled, because nobody will come after this hour till Willis does, and the girls

will be back before that. Willis is to
come and get you on his way to the
Millers', and it's all been arranged for
you, and you needn't think of a thing till
Willis comes. You'll have to dress, of
course ; but you needn't begin that at
once, and you can just sit here in your
chair and rest." Mr. Roberts stretches
his arms wildly abroad, and, throwing
back his head, permits himself a yawn
that eclipses his whole face. Mrs. Roberts lets both her arms fall at her side
in token of extreme despair. "Edward!
If you *should* go to sleep !"

Roberts, pulling himself together, with
a gigantic effort : "No, no! You needn't
be afraid, my dear. But, oh! what
wouldn't I give for a chance to !"

Mrs. Roberts, who sinks into a chair
and regards the unhappy man with a

look of tender compassion: "You poor thing, I've almost a mind to *let* you!"

Roberts, heroically: "No, it wouldn't do, Agnes. I must—ow, ugh, ow—go. Ugh, ow, ugh!" He abandons himself to a succession of abysmal yawns, in which the sequence of his ideas is altogether lost.

Mrs. Roberts: "Well, then, I shall have to trust you." She gathers her train up for departure, and moves slowly towards the door. "I don't think I've forgotten anything. Let me see: fan, handkerchief, both gloves; pins, because you're never sure that they've put enough, and you don't know where you'll come apart; head scarf, yes, I've got that *on;* fur boots, I've got *them* on. I really believe I'm all here. But I shouldn't be, Edward, if it were not for the system I put into everything; and I do wish, dear, that you'd try it once, just to please me!"

Roberts, very drowsily: "Try what, Agnes?"

Mrs. Roberts: "Why, getting what you have to do by heart, and repeating it over. If you could *only* bring yourself to say: *Both girls out; me alone with the children; Willis at ten; mustn't go to sleep; last half, anyway; Mrs. Miller awfully angry.* There! If you could say that after me, I could go feeling so *much* easier! Won't you do it, Edward? I know it has a ridiculous sound, but—"

Roberts, yawning: "How am I to dress?"

Mrs. Roberts: "Edward! Well, I always *will* say that you're perfectly in spired! To think of my forgetting the most important thing, after all! Oh, I do believe there *is* an overruling Providence, I don't *care* what the agnostics pretend. Why, it's to be evening dress for the men, of course! Mrs. Miller would do it to be different from Mrs. Curwen, who let you come in your cutaways, even if it wasn't the regular thing; and she's gone around ever since saying it was the most rowdy, Bohemian thing she ever heard of, and she might as well have had beer, at once."

Roberts : "Who ?"

Mrs. Roberts : "Why, Mrs. Miller."

Roberts : "Mrs. Miller going to have beer ?"

Mrs. Roberts : "Oh, Edward, I don't see how you *can* be so— But there! I won't blame you, dearest. I know you're just literally expiring for want of sleep, and it seems to me I must be the cruellest thing in the world to make you go. And if you'll say the word, I'll smash off a note now at the eleventh hour—though it's two hours of eleven yet!—and just *tell* Mrs. Miller that you've got home down sick, and I've had to stay and take care of you. Will you?"

Roberts: "Oh no, Agnes. It wouldn't be the truth."

Mrs. Roberts, in a rapture of admiration and affection: "Oh, who *cares* for the truth in such a cause, you poor heroic angel, you? Well, if you insist upon going, I suppose we must; and now the only way is for you to keep everything clearly in mind. You'd better say it over backward, now, and begin with evening dress, because that's the most important. Now! *Evening dress; Mrs. Miller awfully angry; last half, any-*

2

*way ; mustn't go to sleep ; Willis at ten ;
me alone with the children ; both girls out.*
Now, do you think— Ow—e—e—e!"
A ring at the door extorts a shriek from
Mrs. Roberts, who simultaneously gathers her robes about her, in order to fall
with decency in the event of burglars or
fire, while her husband rises and goes to
open the apartment door. "Who can it
be, at this hour? Oh! Amy!"

Mrs. Willis Campbell, in the doorway:
"Oh, Amy, indeed! How d' y' do, Edward! Glad to see you back alive, and
just in time for Agnes to kill you with
Mrs. Miller's musicale. May I ask, Agnes, how long you expected me to freeze
to death down in that coupé before you
came?"

Mrs. Roberts: "Oh, Amy, dear, you
must forgive me! I was just staying to

give Edward his charges—you know he's
so terribly forgetful — and I forgot all
about you !"

Mrs. Campbell : "Then I wish, the
next time, he'd give *you* some charges,
my dear. But come, now, do ! We shall
be rather late, anyway, and that simple-
ton will be perfectly furious."

Mrs. Roberts : " Yes, that's just what I
was saying to Edward.   She'll never forgive you.   If it was anybody else, I
shouldn't think of dragging him out to-
night."

Mrs. Campbell : " The worst of a bore
like her is that she's sure to come to all
your things, and you can't get off from
one of hers.   Willis declares he's going
to strike, and I couldn't have got him
out to-night if I hadn't told him you
were going to make Edward go."

Mrs. Roberts: "Oh, isn't it perfectly wicked, Amy! I know he's just going to have the grippe. See how drowsy he is! That's one of the first symptoms."

Mrs. Campbell: "It's one of the symptoms of having passed the night on a sleeping-car, too."

Mrs. Roberts: "That's true, and thank you, Amy. I forgot all about that. But now, Edward, dear, you *will* remember, won't you? If I could only stay with you—"

Roberts, who has been drowsily drooping in his chair during the exchange of these ideas between the ladies: "Oh, I'm all right, Agnes. Or—ow, ugh, ow!—I should be if I had a cup of tea."

Mrs. Roberts: "There! I *knew* it. If I had been worth anything at all as a wife

I should have had you a cup of tea long ago. Oh, how heartless! And I've let both the girls go, and the fire's all out in the range, anyway. But I'll go and start it with my own hands—"

Mrs. Campbell: "In those gloves! You're crazy, Agnes! Edward, I'll tell you what Willis does, when he's out of sorts a little; he takes a taste of whiskey-and-water. He says nothing freshens him up like it."

Roberts: "That's a good idea."

Mrs. Roberts, bustling into the dining-room and reappearing with a tumbler and a decanter: "The very thing, Amy! And thank you *so* much. Trying to make Edward remember seems to put everything out of my head! I might have thought of *whiskey,* though! If it's only loss of sleep, it will wake him up, and if it's grippe, it's the most nourishing thing in the world."

Roberts : "I'm not going to have the grippe, Agnes."

Mrs. Roberts . "Edward ! Don't boast ! You may be stricken down in an instant. I heard of one person who was taken so suddenly she hadn't time to get her things off, and tumbled right on the bed. You must put some water in it, of course ; and hot water is very soothing. You can use some out of the pipes ; it's perfectly good."

Mrs. Campbell : "Agnes, are you *never* coming ?"

Roberts : "Yes, go along, Agnes, do ! I shall get on quite well, now. You needn't wait."

Mrs. Roberts : "Oh, if I could only stay and think *for* you, dearest ! But I can't, and you must do the best you can. Do keep repeating it all over! It's the only way—"

Mrs. Campbell, from the door: "Agnes!"

Mrs. Roberts: "Amy, I'm coming instantly."

Mrs. Campbell: "I declare I shall go without you!"

Mrs. Roberts: "And I shouldn't blame you a bit, Amy! And *if* it turns out to be the grippe, Edward, don't lose an instant. Send for the doctor as fast as the district messenger can fly; give him his car fare, and let one come for me; and jump into bed and cover up warm, and keep up the nourishment with the whiskey; there's another bottle in the sideboard; and perhaps you'd better break a raw egg in it. I heard of one person that they gave three dozen raw eggs a day to in typhoid fever, and even *then* he died ; so you must nourish yourself all you can. And—"

Mrs. Campbell : "Agnes! I'm going!"

Mrs. Roberts : "I'm coming! Edward!"

Roberts : "Well?"

Mrs. Roberts : "There is something else, very important. And I can't think of it!"

Roberts : "Liebig's extract of beef?"

Mrs. Roberts, distractedly : "No, no! And it wasn't oysters, either, though they're very nourishing, too. Oh, dear! What—"

Mrs. Campbell : "Going, Agnes!"

Mrs. Roberts : "Coming, Amy! Try to think of something else that I ought to remember, Edward!"

Roberts: "Some word to the girls when they come in?"

Mrs. Roberts: "No!"

Roberts: "About the children, something?"

Mrs. Roberts: "No, no!"

Roberts: "Willis, then; what Amy wants him to do?"

Mrs. Roberts: "Oh, no, no! I shall surely die if I can't think of it!"

Mrs. Campbell, at the door of the apartment: "Gone!"

Mrs. Roberts, flying after her, as the door closes with a bang: "Oh, Amy! how can you be so heartless? She's driven it quite out of my head!"

3

II

Mr. Willis Campbell: "Hello, hello, hello! *Oh*, hello, hello, hello! Wake up, in there! Roberts, wake up! Sound the loud timbrel! Fire, murder, and sudden death! *Wake* up! Monday morning, you know; here's Tuesday, Wednesday, Thursday, Friday, Saturday, all gone and nothing done! Come, arouse thee, my merry Swiss boy! Take thy pail and to labor away! All aboard! Train for Newton, West Newton, Newtonville, Auburndale, Riverside, and Newton Lower Falls, on track No. 5. Express to Newton. Wake up, Roberts! Here's McIlheny, out here, wants to

know why you took his wife for a cook.
Hurry up! he can't wait. Wake up,
you old seven - by - nine sleeper, you, or
Mrs. Miller's musicale will just simply
expire on the spot. Come! It's after
ten o'clock now, or it will be in about
five minutes. Hurry up! Hello, hello,
hello!" Campbell accompanies his ap-
peals with a tempest of knocks, thumps,
and bangs on the outside of Roberts's
chamber door. Within, Roberts is dis-
covered, at first stretched on his bed
in profound repose, which becomes less
and less perfect as Campbell's blows and
cries penetrate to his consciousness. He
moves, groans, drops back into slumber,
groans again, coughs, sits up on the bed,
where he has thrown himself with all
his clothes on, and listens. "I say,
aren't you going to Mrs. Miller's? If

you are, you'd better get out of bed some time before the last call for breakfast. Now ready in the dining-car!"

Roberts, leaping out of bed and flinging open the door: "Why, I've *been* to Mrs. Miller's!"

Campbell, entering with his hat on, and his overcoat on his arm; "Oh no, you haven't, you poor, suffering creature! That was a heavenly dream! Why, good gracious, man, you're not dressed!" Campbell is himself in perfectly appointed evening-dress, and he stares in dismay at the travelling-suit which Roberts still wears. "You can't go in that figure, you know. You might to Mrs. Curwen's, but you'd give Mrs. Miller deadly offence; she'd think the Curwen had put you up to it. Didn't Agnes tell you I'd be here at ten

for you? What have you been doing
with yourself? I supposed I should find
you walking up and down here, fuming
with impatience."

Roberts : "I was dead tired, and after
Agnes went, I just threw myself down
here for a moment's rest, and I was off
before I knew it—"

Campbell : "Well, then, hustle! There's
no time to lose. We shall be late, but
I guess we can get there in time to save
Agnes's life if we hump ourselves. Are
you shaved?"

Roberts : "Yes, I thought I'd better
shave before I lay down—"

Campbell : "Well, then, that's half the
battle, and you ought to be into your
dress-suit in five minutes; but you're an
intellectual man, and your fingers are all
thumbs, and so I'll give you ten minutes.

Hello! What's this?" In speaking of shaving, Campbell has mechanically cast his eye towards the bureau, and has gradually become aware of the half-tumbler of water and the decanter of whiskey which Roberts has left standing there. He pounces upon the decanter, pulls out the stopple, and applies his nose to the mouth. "Ah, ha! *This* is the milk in the cocoanut, is it? No wonder you slept soundly, and had sweet dreams? Well, Roberts!"

Roberts: "No, no, Willis! I solemnly assure you I haven't touched a drop of it!"

Campbell: "Oh yes! I know! That's what they always say!"

Roberts: "But I tell you, Willis—"

Campbell: "Oh, all right, my boy! I don't blame you! You have never fallen before, probably, but you're down this time, old man. You have every appearance of being grossly intoxicated, as the reporters say, at this instant. Look how red your eyes are!"

Roberts: "It's loss of sleep. I tell you I haven't tasted the whiskey."

Campbell: "But it's half gone!" He lifts the decanter and shows. "Well, I hope Agnes may never know it, and your poor children, Roberts—"

Roberts: "Nonsense! Agnes knows all about it. She brought me the decanter herself. She and Amy thought it would freshen me up. But I distrusted it; I was afraid the effect would be soporific—"

Campbell: "And it seems you were perfectly right. Events have proved it. But come, now, don't sit there all night,

old fellow." Roberts has sunk upon
the edge of the bed. "We've got to be
off to this scene of maddening gayety at
Mrs. Miller's. Want a wet towel round
your head ? Nothing like it, you know !"

Roberts, with dignity : "Thank you, I
don't need any wet towel, and I'll be
with you in a few moments, if you'll
kindly wait." He moves towards the
door of his dressing-room.

Campbell, cheerfully : "Oh, I'll stay
by, Roberts ; you needn't be afraid.
There's nothing mean about me, and
you'll want somebody to pull you together, now and then, and I know just
what to do ; I've been through this kind
of thing with lots of fellows in Califor-
nia. I know the haughty and self-help-
ful stage. You're all right, Roberts.
But don't lose time. What's the matter

now?" Roberts has come back from his dressing-room and is staring vacantly at Campbell.

Roberts : "I was trying to think where I'd put my dress-suit."

Campbell, triumphantly: "Exactly! And *now* do you expect me to believe you haven't been at that decanter? Where do you suppose you put it?"

Roberts : "Where I always do on a hook in my closet."

Campbell . "You hang up your dress-suit? Why, it must look like a butler's! You ought to fold your clothes and lay them in a bureau drawer. Don't you know that? Very likely Agnes has got onto that while you've been away, and put them in here." He looks towards the bureau, and Roberts tries to pull open one drawer after another.

4

Roberts: " This seems locked. I never lock my drawers."

Campbell: " Then that's proof positive that your dress-suit is in there. Agnes has put it in, and locked it up, so as to keep it nice and fresh for you. Where's your key?"

Roberts: " I don't know. I always leave it in the key-hole of one of the drawers. Haven't you got a key-ring, Willis?"

Campbell: " I've got a key-ring, but I haven't got it about me, as Artemus Ward said of his gift for public speaking. It's in my other trousers pockets. Haven't you got a collection of keys? Amy has a half-bushel, and she keeps them in a hand-bag in the bath-room closet. She says Agnes does."

Roberts: "So she does! I'll just look."

While he is gone, Campbell lays down his hat and overcoat, and tries the bureau drawers. Roberts returns to find him at this work. "No; she must have put them somewhere else. I know she always used to put them there."

Campbell: "Well, then we've got to pick the locks. Have you got a boot-buttoner? There's nothing like a boot-buttoner to pick locks. Or, hold on a minute! We've got to go about this thing systematically. Now, I don't think you can tell in your condition whether your dress-coat's in your closet or not, Roberts. We must bring your clothes all out here and lay them on the bed, and see. That dress-suit may turn up yet. You probably thought it was something like an ulster. I know how a man's ideas get mixed, after a little too much freshening up."

Roberts, unmindful of his joke: "You're right, Willis. I may have overlooked it. I'll bring out everything." He disappears, and reappears with a business-suit of black diagonal, which he throws on the bed. "That isn't it."

Campbell, inspecting it: "No; but it isn't so far off. Some of the young chaps have their dress-coats made of diagonal. Try again, Roberts: you'll fetch it yet." Roberts disappears, and reappears with a frock-coat of blue and checked trousers. "Oh, *that* won't do, Roberts. Don't give way like that. Who ever saw a man in evening-dress with check trousers on? Now, what have we next?" As Roberts goes and comes, Campbell receives his burdens and verifies them. "A velvet jacket won't do, either, unless you're a travelling Englishman. Three pairs of summer pantaloons are all very well in their way; but they're out of season, and stripes are not the thing for evening wear any more. Beautiful bath gown, but more adapted for amateur dramatics than for a musicale. Two waistcoats and a Norfolk jacket mean well, but are not adapted to the purpose. Exemplary light overcoat, but still not quite the thing. Double-breasted reefer and Canada homespun trousers; admirably fitted for a sea-voyage and camping out. Armload of semi-detached waistcoats and pantaloons; very suggestive, but not instantly available. Pajamas not at all the thing. Elderly pair of doeskin trousers and low-cut waistcoat

—Why, hello, Roberts! here's part of your dress - suit now! Where's the coat?"

Roberts, dropping into a chair and wiping his forehead, while he surveys the tangled heap of garments on the bed: "Given away. Got too small for me, three years ago. Agnes kept the waistcoat and trousers for the sake of association, because I told her I wore them at the party where we first met. They won't go half round me now."

Campbell, scrutinizing them critically as he holds them : " Well, look here, Roberts, we may have to come to these yet. Stand up, old fellow." Roberts mechanically stands up, and Campbell tries the top of the trousers against his waistband. "May need a little slitting down the back, so as to let them out a third, or two-thirds, or so. But I guess we'll try an ice-pick first." He flings the clothes on the bed, and touches the electric bell.

Roberts : "Ice-pick ?"

Campbell : "Yes; nothing like it for prying open bureau drawers." To Bella, the maid, who appears at the door in answer to his ring: "The ice-pick, please."

Bella : "Ice-pick, sir ?"

Campbell : "Yes. The—ice—pick— here—quick."

Bella, vanishing, with a gesture of wonder at the pile of clothing on the bed: "All right, sir."

Roberts : "But, Willis ! Won't it bruise and deface the bureau ? Agnes is very careful of this bu—"

Campbell : "Not at all. You just set the pick in here over the lock, and pry.

I sha'n't leave a scratch." They stoop
down together in front of the bureau,
and Campbell shows him how. "But
what are you going to do? You've got
to have your clothes if you're going to
the musicale. Ah, here we are! Thanks,"
as Bella comes with the ice-pick, which
he pushes in over the lock of the lowest
drawer. "We'll begin with the lowest,
because that's where Amy keeps mine,
and if Agnes has got onto it through her,
she'll be sure to do exactly the same.
Now, then, I just scratch the bolt down
with my knife, and Open, Sesame! What
do you say to bruising your old bureau
now?"

Roberts, as Campbell pulls out the
drawer and sets it on a chair: "Perfect!
Only"—he lifts the things from the
drawer, and places them on another

chair—"there don't seem to be anything here but underclothes."

Campbell: "Well, then, we must get the next out. No time to lose. Come! Keep shoving the pick in, and I'll scratch the bolt down with my knife. See? It's nothing." They pull the drawer out and set it on the floor, and Roberts ruefully contemplates it.

Roberts: "Nothing but shirts, collars, cuffs and neckties."

Campbell: "Ah, I don't know that. It's a deep drawer"—he begins taking the linen out, and laying it on the floor—"and the dress-suit may be at the bottom. No! Nothing here. You're right, Roberts. Well, now for the top drawer and the last. If we'd taken that out first, we needn't have taken out the second; we could have seen it in place.

You ought to have thought of that, Roberts."

Roberts, with injury: "You suggested taking out the lowest first, yourself, Willis. You said Agnes would be sure to have put them there."

Campbell: "Did I? Well, I knew I must have a reason for it. But come along now, Roberts, and push the ice-pick in." After a season of experiment with the pick and the penknife: "The bolt won't scratch down. What are you going to do now, Roberts?"

Roberts: "I don't know."

Campbell: "But you've got to do something, you know. We can't just give it up. Where are those dress-trousers and waistcoat?" He begins tumbling the things on the bed, laying some on chairs, letting others drop to the floor.

"Ah, here they are! Now, I'll tell you what, Roberts, you've got to wear these. Go into your dressing-room there and put them on, and then we can tell how much they have to be slit up the back."

Roberts: "But where's the coat, even if I could get the other things on?"

Campbell: "We'll think about that later. We haven't got any time to lose in talk. We can pin back the skirts of your frock-coat, as the travelling Americans used to do when they went to the opera in London. Hurry up!" He gives Roberts the garments, and pushes him into the door of his dressing-room, and walks impatiently up and down amidst the chaos of clothing till Roberts reappears. "Why, that isn't bad!"

Roberts: "Bad? I can't breathe; I feel as if I were being cut in two!"

Campbell : " Nonsense! That's the way every woman feels when she's laced. It gives you a beautiful waist, Roberts! Ah, ha, ha, ha! Ha, ha, ha! O Lord! Oh, mercy! Ah, ha, ha, ha!"

Roberts : " Now, look here, Willis—"

Campbell, turning him round, and surveying him from different points: " No, no! Don't mind *me !* It's just my way, you know. I don't mean anything by it. I think these things look first - rate on you. There's no mistake about their giving you a youthful figure; we can just let them out a few stitches, and you'll be perfectly comfortable. The only thing now is the coat. I'm afraid that pinning back wouldn't do. We'd better try something else. I'll tell you! Send down and borrow Merrick's coat! He's still on the floor below you, I suppose?"

Roberts : " Yes, but he's so thin—"

Campbell : " The very thing ! Those thin fellows always have their things made roomy—"

Roberts : " But he's tall."

Campbell : " That's all right. If you keep these things on you've got to give in some direction, and you're probably going to stretch." He rings the bell.

Roberts : " But it's very late. He must be in bed."

Campbell : " I'll fix that." To Bella, as she appears : " Bella, I want you to go down to the gentleman under here, and ask him if he won't lend Mr. Roberts his dress-coat. Tell him Mrs. Roberts has gone off to a party, and Mr. Roberts doesn't know where to find his coat."

Roberts : " Oh, do you think she'd better tell him that, Willis ?"

Campbell: "Why, certainly! You must account for the request in some way. It'll appeal to his sympathy, and put him into a good-humor if he happens to have to get out of bed to oblige you."

Bella: "They're all up yet, sir. I saw their cook on the back stairs when I came in. They've been giving a dinner—"

Campbell: "Well, run then." To Roberts, as Bella vanishes: "Merrick can take it right off his back. But whilst she's gone we'll just give this lock another chance." They work jointly at the bureau drawer. "No, it won't scrape down. It's probably rusted in. You must get this lock oiled, Roberts." As Bella returns with a dress-coat in her hand: "Ah, here we are! That's very nice of Merrick. What did he say?"

Bella: "I didn't see him, sir. The girl brought it."

Campbell: "Well, that's all, Bella." He shakes out the coat as she goes, and looks down at it. "I suppose it amused Merrick. He's got a good deal of humor, Merrick has. I hope he won't give it to the press."

Roberts: "Good heavens, Willis! You don't—"

Campbell: "Oh, he wouldn't give real names. Merrick's too much of a gentleman for that. Come, try it on. We've got to hurry, now." Roberts backs towards him with extended arms and Campbell slips the coat-sleeves on them. "Easy, easy! It may be a little narrow for you in the back— No, sir! It fits you like a glove." He stands off and surveys Roberts, after smoothing the coat across the shoulders. "Yes, sir, like a glove—a glove that the pretty shop-girl has put on for you, after she's peppered it full of that white stuff to make it go on, and told you that you could easily wear a size smaller." He begins to laugh as he lifts each of Roberts's limp arms, with the sleeves dangling below his hands, and touches the skirt, which descends to the calf of his leg. "The most youthful figure I ever saw! Looks like a boy in his father's coat. Merrick *is* a tall fellow. I'd no idea—"

Roberts, looking ruefully over his shoulder: "You see it won't do, Willis."

Campbell: "No, no! I don't say that, quite. But perhaps we'd better try something else. Who's overhead now?"

Roberts, desperately: "Baker. And he's short and fat—"

Campbell: "Short and fat isn't at all bad." Touching the annunciator. "He's probably had his coat made rather long and snug. It'll be the very thing for you. We mustn't leave a stone unturned, or a coat untried." To Bella, appearing at the door, and putting her apron up to control herself at sight of Mr. Roberts's figure: "Do you know whether Mr. Baker's people have gone to bed?"

Bella: "No, sir. I heard their second girl saying on the stairs that Mrs. Baker was up with a bad toothache."

Campbell: "What a piece of luck! Run right up, will you, and borrow Mr. Baker's dress-coat." To Roberts, on Bella's disappearance: "Baker's coat will be all right; but still we'd better work away at this bureau drawer again. Drive the ice-pick in a little farther, now."

6

They struggle with lock as before, until Bella returns, Roberts absent-mindedly keeping Merrick's coat on, and from time to time taking a turn about the room to rest his back.

Roberts: "Let's give it up, Willis. We can't get it open. It's no use!"

Campbell, desisting: "Well, we'll leave that to the last, then. But I've the liveliest confidence in Baker's coat. Ah, here it is! Saved! Saved!" He takes the garment from Bella at the threshold. "Now, then, the great thing is to get Merrick's coat off in one piece. I thought I heard a ripping sound in the back of it when you were straining at that drawer. But I guess it was merely fancy. Easy, easy!" He helps Roberts get the coat off, and examines it.

Roberts, anxiously: "Is it all right?"

Campbell : "Yes, it's perfectly sound. You may have started the seams a little, but it's nothing that Merrick will ever notice. Now for Baker! There! Goes on like an old shoe!" He retires a few steps and surveys Roberts's back, which Roberts is craning his neck round to get a view of in the glass. "*There's* space! Gives you a mighty fine, portly figure, Roberts; it looks *grand* on you, it does indeed! I call that the back of a leading citizen in very comfortable circumstances. Something magisterial about it. Perhaps it's a little full; but that's a good fault; it must set awfully easy. Sleeves are a trifle short, maybe, but not too much to show your cuff-buttons; I hate a coat that don't do that. Yes, I should call that a very nice fit."

Roberts, tearing off the coat, and flinging it on the bed : "You know it won't do, Willis. And now I must give the whole thing up. You'd better hurry off and explain to Agnes why I could not come."

Campbell : "Oh no, I can't leave you in the lurch that way, my dear fellow. Besides it would break Agnes all up. We must *do* something. *I* think either one of those coats would go perfectly well; but if you're so particular about your personal appearance, there's only one thing left. We *must* get this drawer open. Look here. We'll shove the ice-pick in a little farther, so's to give the bolt the slightest possible catch, and then we'll both pull, you on one handle, and I on the other. It won't hurt the bureau. And besides, it's the only chance left. I suppose these coats *don't* look as

"THE SLEEVES ARE A TRIFLE SHORT, MAYBE"

if they were made for you. What do you
say?"

Roberts, disconsolately: "Oh, I suppose
we'd better try. It can't be much worse."
He casts a hopeless glance around the
confused and tumbled room.

Campbell, absently: "Yes. Might as
well be hung for a sheep as a lamb, you
know. Agnes won't be able to express
her feelings anyway when she sees this
room. It looks as if a small cyclone had
been joking round here; but she'll like
your devotion in doing your utmost."

Roberts: "Do you think so? I'm not
so sure. But we'll try it." He pushes
the ice-pick in with all his strength.

Campbell: "That's it! Now then!"
They each grasp a handle of the drawer
and pull. "One, two, three—pull! Once
more—pull! Now the third time—pull!

And *out* she comes !" The bolt suddenly gives and the drawer drops violently
to the floor, scattering its contents in
every direction, while the two men totter
backward and cling to each other to
keep their balance. At the same moment the voices of Mrs. Roberts and
Mrs. Campbell make themselves heard
without in vague cries of astonishment,
question, and apprehension, mounting
into a wild shriek as the drawer crashes
to the floor.

III

Mrs. Roberts, without: "Oh, Edward, *is* it a burglar?"

Mrs. Campbell, without: "Is it a mouse, Willis?"

Mrs. Roberts: "Ring for the district telegraph—call for a policeman, Edward! Press the ratchet down three times!"

Mrs. Campbell: "Don't *kill* him, Willis; don't you *dare* to kill him. Take him up with the tongs and fling him out of the window!"

Mrs. Roberts: "Don't trust him, Edward: get Willis to hold him, and press the ratchet quick!"

Mrs. Campbell: "Keep him from getting back into his hole, for then you never can tell whether he's there or not!"

Mrs. Roberts: "Why don't you answer, Edward? Oh, dear, perhaps he's garroted Edward. I *know* he has!"

Mrs. Campbell: "Willis, if this is any of your tricks—if it's one of your miserable practical jokes—"

Mrs. Roberts: "Oh, I wonder what they're keeping so quiet for! Edward, are you safe? Do you need *me*? If you do, just speak, and I will—go for a policeman, myself!"

Mrs. Campbell: "If you don't answer, Willis—" Whimpering: "Oh, he just wants to make me take my life in my hand! He wouldn't like anything better." The two men, during this rapid colloquy, remain silently aghast, staring at each other and at the scene of confusion around them.

Mrs. Roberts: "Well, then, do it, Amy! You have so much more courage than I have, and you have no children; and if you'll only go to the door and peep in I'll stay here, and keep screaming as loud as ever I can. I'll begin now—"

Roberts: "No, no; don't call out, Agnes. It's all right. We've just had a little accident with one of the bureau drawers. It's perfectly safe; but don't come in till we—" He dashes madly about the room, trying to put it in shape. Both ladies instantly show themselves at the door.

Mrs. Roberts, in dismay at the spectacle: "Why, what in the world has happened, Edward?"

Mrs. Campbell: "It's something Wil-

7

lis has put him up to. I knew it was from the way he kept so still. Where is he?"

Campbell, coming boldly forward out of Roberts's dressing-room, where he had previously taken refuge: "I've saved Roberts's life. If it hadn't been for me he couldn't have moved hand or foot. He was dead asleep when I came here, and I've been helping him look for his dress-suit." At these words Mrs. Roberts abandons herself to despair in one of the chairs overflowing with clothes. "Hello! What's the matter with Agnes?"

Mrs. Roberts: "I never can look any one in the face again! To think of my doing such a thing when I've always prided myself on being so thoughtful, and remembering things so perfectly! And here I've been reproaching Edward

and poor Willis the whole evening for
not coming to that horrid musicale, and
accusing them of all kinds of things,
and all the time I knew I'd forgotten
something and couldn't think what it
was! Oh, dear! I shall simply never
forgive myself! But it was all because
I wanted him to look so nice in it, and I
got it pressed while he was away, and I
folded it up in the tissue-paper myself,
and took the greatest care of it; and
then to have it turn out the way it has!"

Campbell: "What in the world are
you talking about?"

Mrs. Roberts: "Why, Edward's dress-
suit, of course!"

Mrs. Campbell: "Of course she is. But
you always have to have things put in
words of one syllable for you."

Campbell: "No irrelevant insults, Mrs.

Campbell, if you please! Now, Agnes, try to collect yourself. When you had folded his dress-suit in tissue-paper so nicely, what did you do with it?"

Mrs. Roberts: "Why, I wrapped it in my white Chuddah shawl, and put it away back on the top shelf in his closet, and I forgot to tell him where it was." Visible sensation on all sides. "And if Edward were to say now that he couldn't forgive me, I should just simply fall down and worship him."

Campbell: "He can forgive you, probably, but he cannot *forget;* we must leave *that* to women. And here we were, searching every nook and corner of the house, and every hole and cranny, for that dress-suit, which you'd poked away in tissue-paper and Chuddah, while you were enjoying yourself at Mrs. Miller's."

Mrs. Campbell: "We weren't enjoying ourselves. It was the deadliest thing that ever was, and you were very lucky to escape."

Campbell: "That is all very well; but the credit of that belongs entirely to a merciful Providence. What I want to know is how Agnes is going to excuse herself for hiding her husband's clothes, so that if this musicale had been the most delightful affair of the season he would have missed it just the same."

Mrs. Roberts, regarding her husband's strange figure in the youthful waistcoat and trousers: "Why, Edward, dear, what in the world have you got on?"

Campbell: "She doesn't even remember the dress-suit in which poor Roberts first met her! Well, Agnes, you're a pretty wife and mother! Look at that

man!" He takes Roberts by the elbow
and turns him round. "Did you ever
see devotion like that? He's buttoned
in so tight that he can't draw a full breath
to save him, but he would have gone to
the party, if he had expired to slow mu-
sic after he got there; only he couldn't
find the coat. You'd given that away."

Mrs. Campbell, fishing up a garment
from the tempestuous sea of clothes:
"Why, here's a dress-coat, now!"

Campbell: "Yes, that's Merrick's. It
was rather snug for Roberts."

Mrs. Roberts: "And here's another!"

Campbell: "Yes, that's Baker's. It
was rather roomy for Roberts."

Mrs. Roberts: "But how did you get
them?"

Campbell, lightly: "Oh, we sent and
borrowed them."

Roberts, less lightly: "We had to do *something*, Agnes. I knew you would be terribly anxious if I didn't come—"

Mrs. Roberts, with abject contrition: "Oh, don't speak a word, you poor suffering martyr!"

Campbell: "We should have borrowed every coat in the block if you hadn't got back."

Mrs. Campbell: "Yes, and I've no doubt you'd have taken a perfectly fiendish enjoyment in every failure."

Campbell, with a wild, spluttering laugh: "Well, the disappointments certainly had their compensations. Roberts, just let them see how well you look in Merrick's coat! Or, no: try Baker's first; I think Baker's is a little more swell on you, if anything."

Bella, at the door: "Supper is served, Mrs. Roberts."

Campbell: "Supper?"

Mrs. Roberts: "Oh, yes! Mrs. Miller never gives you anything but ice-cream; and I thought we should all need something hot when we got back, and so I had a few— But I forgot all about the supper!"

Campbell: "I'm glad Bella didn't. Better let Bella put Roberts's clothes away, after this."

Mrs. Roberts, in extreme dejection: "Yes, I think I really had, Willis. I'm not fit to be Edward's wife, if I behave that way to him."

Campbell: "Well, well, he must have a divorce, then; but not till after supper."

Mrs. Campbell: "Yes, never mind now, Agnes. It's all turned out well, as it is:

Edward has been spared a fearful bore, and nobody will ever be any the wiser about your putting away his evening dress—"

Campbell : " Oh, indeed ! *Won't* they ? When Baker and Merrick meet at the club, and exchange notes about Agnes locking up Roberts's clothes—"

Mrs. Roberts, with horror : " Edward ! You didn't send that word to them !"

Roberts : " Why—why—I'm afraid we did, something like it, my dear. We had to explain our request, somehow—"

Mrs. Roberts, relaxing into a chair : " Then I simply never can hold up my head again." She lets it fall in typical despair.

Mrs. Campbell, pressing the annunciator, with the energy of a lioness at bay : " I don't believe it's as bad as that. It

8

simply can't be. It would be too abomi-
nable." As Bella appears in answer to
the bell: "Did you tell the gentlemen,
when you went to borrow the coats for
Mr. Roberts, that Mrs. Roberts had
locked up his dress-suit?"

Bella: "Why, that's what Mr. Campbell said to say, ma'am, but I didn't believe Mrs. Roberts would quite like it,
ma'am, and so I said—" She hesitates,
and Mrs. Roberts springs to her feet,
with arms outstretched to her.

Mrs. Roberts: "*What*, Bella?"

Bella: "Why, you know, ma'am, I
couldn't help thinking how things fly
about a house like this."

Mrs. Roberts: "Yes, yes!"

Mrs. Campbell: "Go on!"

Bella: "I didn't believe the gentlemen
would have sent word like that them-

"THAT LITTLE SUPPER"

selves, if they'd thought of it; and so—"

Mrs. Roberts: "And so?"

Mrs. Campbell: "So?"

Bella: "I know you like to have me always speak the truth, and so I do, to you, ma'am, and every lady I ever lived with; but I wasn't going to have that young waitress of Mrs. Baker's and that nasty cook of Mrs. Merrick's laughing at us."

Campbell: "Well, and what did you do?"

Mrs. Roberts: "Yes, Bella!"

Bella: "I told Mrs. Merrick's cook that the gentlemen were getting up some charades; and I told Mr. Baker's second girl that the tailor hadn't sent Mr. Roberts's coat home."

Mrs. Campbell: "Well, you *were* inspired, Bella."

Mrs. Roberts, to Bella: "Oh, you—angel!"

Campbell: "Well, that isn't quite what they call the father of them. Who was the father of what? But we won't dispute about terms. The great thing now is to get at that little supper. Come on, Roberts!"

Mrs. Roberts: "Yes, Edward, take out Amy—"

Roberts, putting himself in evidence: "But don't you see, my dear, I can't draw a full breath now; and if I were to eat anything—"

Mrs. Roberts: "Oh, well, go and change them at once. We won't wait for you, dear, but I'll see to keeping it hot for you."

Campbell, as he follows the ladies out of one door, while Roberts vanishes into

his dressing - room through the other;
"Yes, just slip on anything that will fit
you. It's so near morning now that we
won't insist on evening dress."

THE END